War Stories

T0039603

War Stories

Poems about Long Ago and Now

Howard Nemerov

The University of Chicago Press • Chicago and London

Howard Nemerov is the author of twenty-six books. Eight volumes of his poetry are published by the University of Chicago Press, including *The Collected Poems of Howard Nemerov*, which won the National Book Award and the Pulitzer Prize in 1978. Mr. Nemerov has also been awarded the Bollingen Prize for Poetry, a Guggenheim fellowship, and, recently, the first Aiken Taylor Award for Modern American Poetry. He has been the Edward Mallinckrodt Distinguished University Professor of English at Washington University in St. Louis since 1976.

The University of Chicago Press, Chicago 60637
The University of Chicago Press, Ltd., London

98 97 96 95 94 93 92 91 90   6 5 4 3

Library of Congress Cataloging-in-Publication Data

Nemerov, Howard.
   War stories.

   1. War poetry, American.   I. Title.
PS3527.E5W3   1987   811'.54   87-5097
ISBN 0-226-57242-0 (cloth)
ISBN 0-226-57243-9 (paper)

♾The paper used in this publication meets the minimum requirements of the American National Standard for Information Sciences—Permanence of Paper for Printed Library Materials, ANSI Z39.48-1984.

to Albert & Naomi Lebowitz

The author would like to thank the editors of the following journals for permission to reprint poems first appearing in their pages:

America. "The Shadow Side"
The American Journal of Physics. "To Peter Raven on his Fiftieth Birthday"
The American Poetry Review. "Authorities," "In the Beginning," "The Bluejay and the Mockingbird," "The Celestial Emperor," "The Faith," "IFF," "Intimations," "Playing the Machine"
Expressions. "Fellowship," "The Shopping Mall, The Moral Law"
Harvard Magazine. "The Afterlife," "Models," "World Lines"
The Kenyon Review. "To Dante," "A Reader of Mysteries," "Theater of the Absurd," "Two-Person/Zero-Sum"
The Missouri Review. "Found Poem"
The Paris Review. "Night Operations, Coastal Command RAF," "The War in the Air"
River Styx. "Landscape with Self-Portrait"
The Sewanee Review. "The Biographer's Mandate," "D-Day + All the Years," "Freezing the Rain," "Night Piece," "On Reading *King Lear* Again, 1984," "In Transit"
The Southern Review. "Economic Man," "To Joy our Student, Bidding Adieu," "Low-Level Cross Country," "Parabola," "Remembering the Way"
Southwest Review. "Drowning the Book"
St. Louis Post-Dispatch. "On an Occasion of National Mourning"
The Yale Review. "A Christmas Card of Halley's Comet"

His thanks also to Sharon Bangert for typing the fair copy, the revised fair copy, and what is hoped to be the fairest copy of all.

Contents

1 The War in the Streets

To Joy Our Student, Bidding Adieu

Your friends, dear woman whom I never knew
But by the delighted kindness of your smile,
Impersonal but kindness and delight
Received and like a blessing on the day,
Had got accustomed to the thought of death
As age and preparation and farewell,
With things to settle, time to settle things
Before we left; now you've surprised us
As you had scarce the time to be surprised,
Leaving the company and the lighted room
With the wine and warmth and amiable talk
To go home in darkness, on the rainy roads,
To cross the avenue none gets across—

But suddenly, my dear, struck off the books,
Gone missing in the middle of the way
For time's remainder, such as it may be.
Remembering your smile, I wish that I
Had learned it better, and got it down by heart,
That no more lights the narrow hall of day
With all your troubled kindness, your delight.

Intimations

Alan Turing's Imitation Game,
Where the artifice of intelligence began,
Turned in the first place on a single theme:
How can you tell a woman from a man?

Alas, life imitates not only art
But science too. They can't be told apart.

The Royal Visit

There will be fountains shaking aloft their plumes,
And fireworks to lift away the night
(all will go "ooh!" at the soaring against gravity
and "ahh!" at the bursting drift against the night),

There will be revelry, licensed misrule
Under the indulgent eyes of the police,
And waltzing in the streets after the long
Parade adorned with allegorical girls

On flowered floats postured and postulant
To signify, between the marching bands,
Order, The State, War, Victory, and the Arts,
When the Prince rides through the city in arms,

He will pardon the thieves and murderers,
Empty asylums and jails into the streets,
The city and the world will be renewed,
He will leave in splendor through the western gate.

Ultima Ratio Reagan

The reason we do not learn from history is
Because we are not the people who learned last time.

Because we are not the same people as them
That fed our sons and honor to Vietnam
And dropped the burning money on their trees,

We know that we know better than they knew,
And history will not blame us if once again
The light at the end of the tunnel is the train.

Authorities

Commanders, and behind them heads of state,
Are said to care for and spend sleepless nights
About the children they commit to war;
You can't help wondering, though, whether they do

Or whether, were you safely in their place
Of power, as it's not likely you would be
Nor weren't, but it's allowed to wonder,
You might not say, "Poor bastards, little shits,

They never learned their history in schools
And now they never will, and cannot know
They are the hinges on which the oily valves
Of history will balance before they close

Upon our reputations now, our fame
In aftertimes, when children will be schooled
Again in truths belatedly belied,
To shoulder our burden and their hopeless charge."

At Sixties and Seventies

Anything goes! they cried incontinent.
And sure as death and taxes, everything went.

Let it all hang out, they used to say,
Who cannot stuff it all back in to stay.

Forgetting the rule about reaping what is sown:
First live it up, then try to live it down.

On An Occasion of National Mourning

It is admittedly difficult for a whole
Nation to mourn and be seen to do so, but
It can be done, the silvery platitudes
Were waiting in their silos for just such
An emergent occasion, cards of sympathy
From heads of state were long ago prepared
For launching and are bounced around the world
From satellites at near the speed of light,
The divine services are telecast
From the home towns, children are interviewed
And say politely, gravely, how sorry they are,

And in a week or so the thing is done,
The sea gives up its bits and pieces and
The investigating board pinpoints the cause
By inspecting bits and pieces, nothing of the sort
Can ever happen again, the prescribed course
Of tragedy is run through omen to amen
As in a play, the nation rises again
Reborn of grief and ready to seek the stars;
Remembering the shuttle, forgetting the loom.

Crotchets

I

The Man in the Street

One thing I don't like most in the world, he said,
Is these creeps walking around wired for sound
With the dumb expressions on the faces like
They was out of this world, no way to tell
What kind of thing them boxes on the belts
Are putting between their ears, might be from Mars
Or Moscow for all you know, zombies like them
Should get themselves run over crossing the street.

II

At Breakfast this Morning

She tells me out of the paper about this guy
He's got leukemia and into the bargain AIDS,
They give him maybe two more weeks to live
When the oxygen tank outside the room explodes
And he winds up in emergency and then
Intensive care all over third-degree burns.
But they saved his life, they brought him back.

So don't try to, she says, tell me there is no God.

Happy Hour

Here, on the way from source to sink,
Between the brewery and the piss,
The pale already golden drink,
The dream, the kindness, the company, and the kiss.

The Shopping Mall, the Moral Law

The mannequins, young visions of delight
Outfitted all for sporting and for sports,
Lean back a bit with breast and thigh outthrust
In lazily yielding postures that invite
Into their filmy designers' shirts and shorts.

To stabilize their stance and prop upright
These swooning figures of a plastic lust
And keep them coming to this pretty pass
Without arriving, a discipline of sorts
Makes sure each has a ramrod up her ass.

Found Poem

after information received
in The St. Louis Post-Dispatch,
4 v 86

The population center of the USA
Has shifted to Potosi, in Missouri.

The calculation employed by authorities
In arriving at this dislocation assumes

That the country is a geometric plane,
Perfectly flat, and that every citizen,

Including those in Alaska and Hawaii
And the District of Columbia, weighs the same;

So that, given these simple presuppositions,
The entire bulk and spread of all the people

Should theoretically balance on the point
Of a needle under Potosi in Missouri

Where no one is residing nowadays
But the watchman over an abandoned mine

Whence the company got the lead out and left.
"It gets pretty lonely here," he says, "at night."

Fellowship

"Be generous and delicate and pursue the prize"
    —Henry James, Jr.

The winners have, as written, their reward,
But sulk not, losers, take it not so hard,
For a thousand elderly hacks like these and me
The true annuity to this award
Is Hope reinstigated in the heart
That next year, or in some year yet to be,
By a Last Judgment just as it is strict,
We shall be lifted up and set apart.

No matter, meanwhile, that we die unpick't
With all our sweetness left to ripe and rot;
What is to come must come from what is not,
And we may yet get in Pandora's *boîte*.

Playing the Machine

You open P-K4, it thinks, or blinks,
For thirty seconds and answers with the same.
It's merciless with tactical mistakes,
Perfected at following the game's First Law,
Bother The Enemy, deploys its forces
Faster and better than you do because
It threatens you with this while you think that
And that while you think this; you sacrifice
A willing pawn to get mobility,
Before you notice it snaps up two pawns more;
It knows where the second bishop ought to go
While you're still thinking how like love that is
(where do you put the other arm?), and so
It ought to wipe up the board with you every time.

But something intervenes, maybe the maker
Complaining to the programmer: "If you won't
Allow the schlemiels to win one now and then
How will I sell your dumb machine?"

So unexpectedly it puts its queen *en prise*
And leaves it there, or castles into mate,
Making you wonder if you really won
Or if its circuits, trying to imitate
The true stupidity of the human mind,
Became recursive and put it into doubt.

15

But up at Level Seven, or so say
The instructions, it enters The Infinite Mode
Where it will think deeper and deeper still
Until you press it to stop and make its move
Whatever—or you can always turn it off,
Declare a victory and leave it there,
Somewhat the way you leave a telling dream,
Taking its faithless memory away.

The Biographer's Mandate

Of course he became famous toward the end,
And a little bit rich, or else you wouldn't be
Writing his life. We know he wrote the books,

But now let's have the dirty worst. Was he
Closetly gay? Transvestite? Into s
& m? Or ever in trouble with the law?

His normals, too. Number of infidelities,
The long liaisons and the one-night stands?
And were they important people like he was?

As well as money and celebrity:
Advances, movie contracts, royalties;
Did he lunch with producers, did he dance with stars?

For we don't give a shit about his work.
These are the things we give a shit about.

Parabola

". . . it is difficult to comprehend the Generals' losing streak. The Harlem Globetrotters' opponents have lost more than 4,000 consecutive games. . ."
  —Alex Nemerov, in *The Vermont Cynic* for 25 x 84

For the acknowledged masters of the court
To show their stuff, they need a victim team
Superbly skilled, dispassionate, well-paid,
Their goodness a sacrifice to excellence
Night after night, night after long night.

No matter how well they play, and they play well,
They always lose, and look good doing it.
They are professionals who know their job,
Which is to lose and look good doing it.
You've got to admire the stoical guts it takes
To go out there every night and lose for a living,

Though a losing streak four thousand agons long
Is also impressive, belongs in The Book of Records,
Teaches humility, persistive constancy
And other excellent virtues to the kids who watch
And learn how grown men face the life of loss.

The oldest Generals remember a game they won,
When somebody hit the rim and the ball fell in
In the final second of play, instead of out
As it was meant to do. No one was blamed
For the kind of fluke that could happen to anyone,
"But it got kind of quiet in the stands."

Commencement

Arthur and Dennis, Karen, Gene, and Joy,
Our earliest graduates, examined by
Boredom, Despair, Accident, Heredity
The ancestors' preemptive strike. They passed.

The Bluejay and the Mockingbird

The mockingbird, knowing he owned the tree,
Flew close on the tail of an interloper jay.
Through and around they went one after one
With considerable skill not hitting a branch
Nor even it seemed disturbing a single leaf,
And neither left the precinct of the tree.

For all we're told of territoriality,
There was no pecking, they seemed to be having fun
Of a serious sort; at intervals agreed
Each one retired to a neutral branch,
Where the bluejay screamed and the mockingbird copied him.

Drowning the Book

"Life is hard. And then you die."

Now listen, Howie, if anyone ever read
Those little verses that you sometimes do,
It wouldn't have been because they wanted to hear
About age, old age, and illness, and the grave
Or all that there they know enough about
Without your help, without your dubious help.

There's but three steps from Milton back to malt,
And but three grains of salt with a peck of dirt
Between the elegant this and the silly that;
And the purpose of poesy, as all of us know
Without the sermon, is, by telling the truth,
To disintoxicate and disenchant
By lying like Homer taught us first to do.

You'll recollect what in this vale of tears
Is consequent, that there are girls in it
Lighting desires that a bachelor sage
Said God alone could satisfy (He sometimes does),
Moving the way they move in dithery
Delight, with the delicate bend and thrust
Of this and that about their splendid persons

The sentiment of the epigraph would have been unremarkable enough save that
when first seen it covered both points on a T-shirt. The known instructors, with a

Until they swell and cry aloud for corks
And fade into the light of common day
To start our burning busyness again—

And why would they give a fart in a high wind
When every wheel of this unwearied mill
That turned ten thousand verses . . . this living hand?
You made your bargain before you made your bed:
Lie in it still, as if you must you may.

---

long life's gratitude, are: William Shakespeare, T. H. White, John Milton, A. E. Housman, John Keats, W. H. Auden, Aristotle for Homer, Henry Thoreau, Alexander Pope, William Wordsworth, William Yeats, and, of course, John Keats again.

2 The War in the Air

Models

1.

The boy of twelve, shaping a fuselage
Of balsa wood so easy to be sliced
Along the grain but likely to get crushed
Under the razor when it was cut across;

Sanding the parts, glueing and lacquering
And pasting on the crosses and the rings
The brave identities of Fokker and Spad
That fought, only a little before his birth,

That primitive, original war in the air
He made in miniature and flew by hand
In clumsy combat, simulated buzz:
A decade away from being there himself.

2.

The fuselage in the factory was aligned on North
So that the molecules lay along the axis,
Or so they said, to make the compass read
A right magnetic course; and after an attack

You headed the aircraft to what you hoped was North
And fired one more burst at the empty night
To set the shaken compass true again:
It straightened the molecules, or so they said.

The broken circle with the centered cross
Projecting the image at infinity
Quivered before him in the vacant air
Till it lay on the target like a haloing light.

3.

And memory, that makes things miniature
And far away, and fit size for the mind,
Returned him in the form of images
The size of flies, his doings in those days

With theirs, the heroes that came out of the sun
To invent the avant-garde war of the air—
Richtofen, Rickenbacker, and the rest—
Where if you were shot it would be in the back,

Where the survivors, by their likenesses
Before and after, aged decades in a year,
Cruel-mouthed and harsh, and thought the young recruit
Not worth their welcome, as unlike to last.

Low-Level Cross-Country

for Brooks Baekeland

A railroad and a river and a road
Roughly in parallel though near and far
By turns and sometimes twisted in a thread

Three-ply with crossings-over, tunnelings-in,
And passing astern as soon as coming up,
With every slope and slippage of terrain—

And suddenly the town has been and gone,
The market square, the churches, and the schools,
The cemeteries and the swimming pools,

And out again, map folded on one knee
To read ahead, if there were time to read
With all the names aslant or upside down,

And over the rises and the deep ravines
Uncharted, lonely, still, and left behind
In the steady passage of the exercise

At the scope of speed and the escape of space
Down on the deck, perplexities resolved
Before they can be solved, and all the world

Flowing away the way it always does,
As if it were made of time, the thrice-wound theme
Of the railroad and the river and the road.

Night Operations, Coastal Command RAF

Remembering that war, I'd near believe
We didn't need the enemy, with whom
Our dark encounters were confused and few
And quickly done, so many of our lot
Did for themselves in folly and misfortune.

Some hit our own barrage balloons, and some
Tripped over power lines, coming in low;
Some swung on takeoff, others overshot,
And two or three forgot to lower the wheels.

There were those that flew the bearing for the course
And flew away forever; and the happy few
That homed on Venus sinking beyond the sea
In fading certitude. For all the skill,
For all the time of training, you might take
The hundred steps in darkness, not the next.

IFF

1.

Hate Hitler? No, I spared him hardly a thought.
But Corporal Irmin, first, and later on
The O.C.(Flying), Wing Commander Briggs,
And the station C.O. Group Captain Ormery—
Now there were men were objects fit to hate,
Hitler a moustache and a little curl
In the middle of his forehead, whereas these
Bastards were bastards in your daily life,
With Power in their pleasure, smile or frown.

2.

Not to forget my navigator Bert,
Who shyly explained to me that the Jews
Were ruining England and Hitler might be wrong
But he had the right idea . . . We were a crew,
And went on so, the one pair left alive
Of a dozen that chose each other flipping coins
At the OTU, but spoke no civil word
Thereafter, beyond the words that had to do
With the drill for going out and getting back.

IFF = Identification Friend or Foe, a signalling device carried on aircraft for that
        purpose
OTU = Operational Training Unit

3.

One night, with a dozen squadrons coming home
To Manston, the tower gave us orbit and height
To wait our turn in their lofty waiting-room,
And on every circuit, when we crossed the Thames,
Our gunners in the estuary below
Loosed off a couple of dozen rounds on spec,
Defending the Commonwealth as detailed to do,
Their lazy lights so slow, then whipping past.
All the above were friends. And then the foe.

The War in the Air

For a saving grace, we didn't see our dead,
Who rarely bothered coming home to die
But simply stayed away out there
In the clean war, the war in the air.

Seldom the ghosts came back bearing their tales
Of hitting the earth, the incompressible sea,
But stayed up there in the relative wind,
Shades fading in the mind,

Who had no graves but only epitaphs
Where never so many spoke for never so few:
Per ardua, said the partisans of Mars,
Per aspera, to the stars.

That was the good war, the war we won
As if there were no death, for goodness' sake,
With the help of the losers we left out there
In the air, in the empty air.

The Faith

"There are those for whom war is a vocation. . . . They are mystic
soldiers, devout—and killing is their calling. What of them?"
    —Kenneth Burke

I knew a couple of these dedicates,
The ones that loved the life and volunteered
For more of it after they'd got home free
And honorably discharged with all the gongs.

A strange pair if they ever were a pair
Save in my thought, they never knew each other
Far as I knew though they behaved the same
In combat, coldly reckless and extreme,

Although not out of it: for one was mild
And modest, but the other cantankerous
And insubordinate, was once torn off a strip
Same day as decorated for the same deed.

One aimed his aircraft at a battle cruiser
(it turned out one of ours) and was blown away;
The other signalled from behind the Frisians
That he and his crew were hit and going down,

His voice as neutral as the evening news
That we would hear on our return to base
That night: "From these and other operations
Seven of our aircraft failed to return."

They were the heroes, we others carried the spears
In the war that in the last place had been won
By the duty-bound, the neither more nor less.
And now I can't remember which was which.

Double Negative

old pilot to new

"Hours of boredom, minutes in mortal range,
Then twenty seconds as a helpless mark,
A target yourself while targeting the kill,
You start your cannons going going in
Though far too far away to count, because
The bullets going out are a guarantee
Of sorts against the bullets coming in.
A magical idea? But just as much
A law of nature, your own nature I mean,
As if you found it in a physics book.

"Nor don't you imagine, when during your dive,
As it's almost bound to happen, one of your chaps
Crosses his aircraft over in front of yours
Between your gunsight and the sitting ship
—plenty adrenalin then, instead of fear—,
You won't keep pressing your pale-knuckled thumb
Down on that button. I know it for a fact,
And sank the ship that day, and got my gong,"
Fingering the ribbon there, the striped purple and white
Over his heart and underneath his wings.

World Lines

A War Story

And there I was, is how these things begin,
Doing my final exam, a solo test
Of navigation by dead reckoning;
If you got there and back, you had to pass.

I got there in good shape, a mining town
Far north of nowheresville, and had turned for home
When the cloud closed down and the snow swept in,
Nothing but speeding snow and darkness white,

But I found the spur of a railroad headed south,
The Iron Compass, the Lost Flyer's Friend,
And followed that at a couple of hundred feet
Until it tunneled into the side of a hill,

And there I was. What then? What happened then?
Now who was I to know what happened then,
A kid just out of school the year before?
His buttons and bones are somewhere out there still.

Memorial Day, '86

D-Day + *All the Years*

What Daddy did on Opening Day? Yes, well,
He led the squadron out before first light
Over the Channel as far as Cap Gris Nez
And turned to port along the Frisian shores
Up past Den Helder and Terschelling where
We had lost a few, and so on up as far
As the Bight of Heligoland and distant Denmark
Where Hamlet and the others used to live,
And so wheeled homeward on a parallel track
To land at Manston in Kent for an early lunch.

Pleasant and warm under the perspex canopy
Of the office fifty feet above a sea
Hammered and brazen as on the world's first day,
A peaceable morning. And the sky was blue.

And Daddy sitting there driving along
Under his silly hat with the stiffener out,
Wearing the leather gauntlets flared heroic
Over the white silk elbow-length debutante's gloves
They used to wear then whatever the weather was,
And more or less the way you see him now.

Remembering the Way

When you get to where you're going after dark,
To the strange house where a shadowy person behind
A lantern lights you to an upstairs room,
You drop your kit and undress in the dark
And haven't anything to do but sleep
Or fail to sleep until the dawn lights up
And you can see what you have come to, this
Bare room that will be your room from now on
With its one window opening out upon
The lawn and thence to the field falling away
To the river shining between the trees and last
To the hills that rise beyond.
                              It happened that way
During the war sometimes, when you were posted
To a new place and got there after dark.

The Shadow Side

The evening sunlight coming down the meadow
And slanting through the window strikes to light
A silver service that her father sent
Down from the Enlightenment and across the sea
To cast its complicities of light and shadow
On the white wall in halo and silhouette.

Some things remain the same, the silver bowls
And swan-necked coffee urn with the fluted sides,
But shift their shapes now as their shadows pass
Along the wall, while evening on the meadow
And evening in the room make indistinct
The silver highlights sinking into gloom

Until it is full night and the new-made widow
Remains unmoved and dark and derelict
In the museum of wreckage and regret
Left of a life subjected to earth's shadow.

The Afterlife

The many of us that came through the war
Unwounded and set free in Forty-Five
Already understood the afterlife
We'd learned enough to wait for, not expect,
During the years of boredom, fear, fatigue;
And now, an hour's worth of afterlife.

Fort Dix, there at the gate, boarding the bus
That let me off in Newark to catch a train
That took me to Penn Station and left me there
Once more the young man on his own and free
Without much money, and with not much to do:
The Gates of Paradise opened and let me out.

In the real one, as I understand it now,
They'll take you to a base camp far from home
And line you up for uniforms and shots
And scream incomprehensible commands
Until you learn obedience again.
It will feel strange at first. But so it goes.

3 The War in the Heavens

In the Beginning

Thus Freud deposed about our infant state:
Omnipotent and impotent at once;
Wawl and it shall be given.

Though what is given is never what we want,
So we must wawl again. O chiefs of state,
Are you like this, like us in this?

And God, you holy terror
With the big bang for the buck,
Are you as ourselves in this also?

Like any terrorist making all things new
Including the freedom of the will and the huge
Unsuitable purple hat

Aunt Sadie wore to sister's wedding?
And this verse also, was it there
When the morning stars sang together

And the other celebrities shouted for joy?
And is that why the infant in the crib,
Bearing revenge's infancy, condemned
To suck his thumbs till able to bite his nails,
Hollered like Freud among the cattle and kings?

More Joy in Heaven

This bird that a cat sprang loose in the house,
Still flyably warm and wet from the cat's mouth,
Beat like a heart set fluttering with fear;
The bird's heart first, but ours beat after it.

Some comedy came of this, the saner sort
Opening doors, the others batting at cats
With brooms, or flying towels at the bird
To muffle it safe from enemy and self;

Who after getting confused among the drapes
And flopping back from a window, from a wall,
Found out the empty daylight of a door
Left open, and left, thinking the good thoughts

It would tell its children in our children's books
About an ultimate kindness to the world
Where once, in a legend of the Golden Age,
One ecosystem beat the other, once.

Economic Man

for Naomi Lebowitz

He would have liked to find a use for leaves,
So simple a thing it seemed, so many of them
Flying and falling, going to waste and wet
And stopping up the gutters and the drains
Or drying in the still November days
Until swept into heaps, gone up in smoke
As if all summer's shade had never been.

And so he dreamed, and idly enough,
For many summers, many falls, until
His spell upon the earth was done, come time
To fall, while the useless leaves still came and went,
And the green had told him nothing, nor the sere,
That he might leave for men to profit by.

Two-Person/Zero-Sum

The serious boy playing himself at chess
Always contrives to win, but subtly enough
That his obliging loser across the board
Will never realize what made him make
The plausible insignificant mistake
That would lead to loss in a dozen moves or so,

Nor ever thinks to assign a face or name
To the invisible other who is always there
Accepting the consequences of his acts
In stoical silence, subtly playing to lose
To the self on the hither side playing himself.

Thus do they even to the end of life.

In Transit

An apple tree past bearing stands before
A willow already weeping her early gold;
Behind them, topping both, an evergreen,
All three in transit or in line astern.

Dame Kind, I see, is drawing a diagram,
Speaking in parable as she generally does,
This one of thee and me and someone else
Unknown, in triangle or in trinity.

I stand before them, absently entranced,
Until I shudder from the cold March wind,
Daydreaming winter and spring and some third thing;
Cold spring, that keeps the flowering slow and long.

Theater of the Absurd

Strange is the show enacted in the cave
Alone, whereat the unassisted man,
Lying as dead, does nothing on his own
Yet is responsible for all that's done,

Inventing the music as he sings the song,
Author, director, playing all the parts;
Forbidden to applaud or fall asleep,
He is sole audience to the moving scene

He cannot interrupt, revise, control,
Only endure to the arbitrary end
And curtain-rise upon the other world,
Removing what he like as not forgets.

To Peter Raven on his Fiftieth Birthday

One iris'd feather of a mallard's wing
Here on the table in fluorescent light,
Its delicately curving parallels
Of thin hairs closely stitched and springing from
The tapering cambered spine that is so hard
Though hollow, and still flexible for flight,

I delight to see it and inscribe it so,
While figuring its form intrinsicate
As of the selfsame nature with the one
That gave me the sense to see it as it is
Along with mind to know it as it isn't,
And neither of us meaning one blessed thing.

Night Piece

His winter robe across an arm of the chair
In the night-light coming from the closet door
(because a cat had taken to sleeping there
in its furred and carpeted senility)
Reminded him, by the fallen folds of brown
Cloth wrinkling gold one way and black another
As sand dunes do in nearly level light,
Of whom? What was the painter's wretched name?

Spanish and simple, with St. Francis cowled,
Faceless and sinister, absent as near as not
Under the single source of concealing light?
In the cat's cradle of liquid and sibilant,
Murillo . . . Velázquez . . . something beginning in V?
No, neither of those, though he was coming close,
Till a door slid open and told him Zurbarán
And he smiled for happpiness and fell asleep.

Freezing the Rain

Ice over ice, ice over snow,
Song of the few degrees
Of difference in the winter's weather,
Coefficient of friction down near zero
And the city gone inanimate.

Like weightlessness in space
With gravity gone while mass remains,
It changes the heft of bodies,
Balance and the power of the will
Gone glimmering, gone downhill,

With cars abandoned in unlikely places,
And hapless people on their coated rumps
Gliding where gravity would have them glide,
Down to the sump of the street
Where they oscillate a bit
Till they bottom out and wait
For help to share their fate.

A world might gather there
Waving its legs, before the end,
Before things mend.

A Reader of Mysteries

"a book too mad to read
Before one merely reads to pass the time."

He reads to pass the time, and it seems to work:
Time passes. Often as not, he reads in bed
In the winter evenings at the edge of sleep,
Aware of the digital clock across the room
Sending him numbers in an emerald light
Remindful of the tomb.
                    The mysteries he reads
Are soothing to death, which now is not the end
But the beginning, the motive and the spring
For all succeeding, as the psychopomp
Follows the unknown through the labyrinth
Solving for x and blackboarding to the group,
Until in a secret chamber of the dream
He meets and renders up his minotaur.

This is recurrent with him, and if sleep
Has not arrested him before the end
He starts another, still unsatisfied
And often enough unable to understand
Or even to remember the extravagant
Unscrambling of the false appearances
Or merely to see the little numbering light
Of the revealed truth. Very like life itself,
He tells himself, as the addictive drug
Takes hold and sleep comes down to overcome;
Very like death itself, his murder done—
Maybe be taken in the middle of one
Unsolved, and never do find out who done it.

On Reading King Lear Again, 1984

After the many things it's been about,
Maybe the one last thing *King Lear's* about
Is God's way with his people and the world.

The white-haired widower's classic double-bind,
"How much do you love me?" against "I want the truth,"
Where flattery is required and the truth outlawed,

Is like the prayer demanded of the prey,
"Now tell me what you really think of me,
Before I kill you anyhow." Critics

Who cast Cordelia as "a type of Christ"
Should honor the obligation they incur
To all the story, not just part of it.

The god who gives the world away to kids
Will go a long road and a rainy night
Before his wits give way and he forgives.

The Celestial Emperor

Against the invisible antagonist
Waiting across the squared-off court below,
The emperor plays chess with living men,
The pieces all convicted criminals
For economy's sake already sentenced to die,
Which happens to them as they're sacrificed,
Exchanged, or merely lost by accident,
The emperor's or his enemy's misplay.

The men go through the motions as they're moved,
Moaning or sighing as the gambit goes,
And some, that are left in play for long enough,
Become connoisseurs and critics of the game
With exclamation point or question mark
As they approve or disapprove the choice.
He hears them not nor heeds, but listens to
The music of his clockwork nightingale

Immortally singing the fashionable songs
That imitate our planetary fates
Moving against a figured ground of stars
That are fixed and firm as he, and never moved.
So many destinies are in the world
That to each of them the appointed child is born;
Though God be dead, he lived so far away
His sourceless light continues to fall on us.

To Dante

To write an epic with an all-star cast,
Even the extras somebodies in their day,
To have for theme the whole of history
With plenty to spare, to finish all that up
By falling asleep in the divine mind
And disremembering everything at once,
With everyone you ever knew, as well
As everyone you ever didn't, dead;
You on that stage to be the only one
Alive among the crowding shadows, well,
We always figured that's what poets want,
And by God you got it, the whole damned blessed lot.

How lonely, though, between the eternities,
The long way down, and up, and over and out.

A Christmas Card of Halley's Comet

The fast and faint and temporary star,
Dragging the streak of tail that in our comic books
Is the artist's way of representing speed,

Heads out diagonally across the field
Of royal blue darkness with some specks of stars,
Where, absent the beasts, the shepherds, and the kings,

The unmanned universe remains, traversed
By this ice-blue burning snowball that returns
At the interval of an aged person's life

And wastes the rest of time crossing the vast
That separates one nothing from the next.
Words fail us, and The Word, that failed before.

All Things Made New for Now

Come down from Portland on the early flight
To Boston over Massachusetts Bay,
Across the water's wrinkled skin, the odd
Ship spreading its wake, there in the risen light
On the left came up the crooked wrist of sand,
Provincetown's tower, the lighthouse on Race Point—

So far apart by road, so near by sky—

How close together and small his early world
So suddenly became itself again,
Familiar and miniature under the eye
Of the grown-up riding high in memory
Of summers come and summers gone, to change
At Logan and head on home, far from the sea.

Landscape with Self-Portrait

A shading porch, that's open to the west
Whence the weather comes, and giving on a lawn
Won from the meadow where the hay's been baled
In cubes like building blocks of dusty gold,
And further down, through trees, the streaming creek
With three still pools by passagework
Of rapids and rills in fretted rhythms linked;

And on the porch the life-defeated self
And reciprocating engine of reverie
Translating to time the back and forth of space,
The foot's escapement measuring the mind
In memories while the whole antic machine
Precesses across the floor and towards the edge
And has to be hitched back from time to time;

And there to watch the tarnished silver cloud
Advancing up the valley on a wind
That shudders the leaves and turns them silverside
While shadows sweep over stubble and grass,
And sudden the heavy silver of the first
Raindrops blown slanting in and summer cold
And turning continuous in silver strings;

And after that, the clarified serene
Of the little of daylight that remains to make
Distinct the details of the fading sight:
The laddered blue on blue of the bluejay's tail,
The sweeping swallows low above the swale
Among the insect victims as they rise
To be picked off, and peace is satisfied.